The Regulator-Moderator War of East Texas

A Family Story

Edward Hancock II

ISBN: 979-8-774-43792-4

DEDICATION

Dedicated to all the maternal ancestors and relatives that did not live to see this project come to life. Those who participated in the Regulator-Moderator War and those who descended from them. May these stories help us all to live eternal... and in peace.

INTRODUCTION

If someone said the word "Regulators" to you, chances are good your mind would journey back to an 80's western movie starring the likes of Kiefer Sutherland, Emilio Estevez and Charlie Sheen. You'd be forgiven for not knowing that the very real events depicted in that fictional adventure took place 30 years after another conflict in which a team of Regulators fought a group – the Moderators – for power and influence and, as the name implied – regulation of land swindlers and other characters they deemed unsavory, such as Joseph Goodbread. Unlike the New Mexico conflict of the 1870's, this conflict would envelop much of modern-day Northeast Texas including a strip of border lands between the Lone Star State and the contemporary territory belonging to Louisiana. This strip of land was known by many names, including the Sabine Free State and, more simply, Neutral Ground. Unfortunately, the ground was anything but neutral, though it was difficult to find anywhere the factions known as the Regulators and Moderators weren't willing to fight.

This is a story about a little-known period in Texas history. More than that, it is the all-too-personal story of 5 men – 4 men from whom the author directly descends, one distant granduncle. It is the story of a literal civil war among cattle rustlers, land grabbers, bullies and those bent on curtailing their efforts, by whatever means necessary. Too, it is the story of two factions resolved to eliminate each other and the Texas government determined to put an end to the fighting, if only to protect the effort toward American annexation.

As of this original first edition, there's no solid evidence any of the five men depicted here had much more than a general familiarity with one another. A story exists wherein two of the men may have had an exchange of gunfire, as they were on opposing sides, but the details are wholly unclear how far their familiarity with each other truly went. Did they know each other? Were they great friends, only to become bitter enemies? Did they attend the same church or work in the same lumber yards or shops? As of this writing, no personal correspondence of the men can be referenced to verify or refute any strong relation or knowledge that might have existed among these men, save the father and son that participated as part of the Regulator faction. At least one was probably a stranger to the others. (Though that's admittedly speculation based on very limited evidence available at the time of this writing.) Later, two descendants of those involved in the fighting married, leading to many descendants, including the author.

This book has taken literal years to research, navigate, outline and, finally, write. (Honestly, the writing part has been the quickest aspect of the entire process.) The people involved in this book's creation have waded through false leads, gone down intense rabbit trails and gone back and forth as to what information was worthy of inclusion and what was superfluous in the accurate and complete telling of my family's involvement in and connection to the Regulator-Moderator War of Shelby County, Texas. There are a surprising number of books, articles and websites devoted to the Regulator-Moderator War as a whole. To date, the team involved in researching this work has only encountered one writing that recounted the tale from the perspective of those involved in this conflict. Another told the tale second hand from the descendant of one of the participants. None of those known recollections are by any of the men depicted here, nor by their known relatives.

First and foremost, to relegate this war to one Texas county is factually inaccurate. People from at least 4 Texas counties participated in this conflict and at least one person would travel as far away as Louisiana in hopes of avoiding the violent fate met by many of his friends and associates.

The principle leaders during much of the hostilities were Charles W. Jackson and Charles W. Moorman for the Regulators and Edward Merchant, John M. Bradley, and James J. Cravens for the Moderators. Their differences can be traced back to land frauds, cattle rustling, barn burners, and revenge killings. Dozens were killed between 1839 and 1844. With seemingly no end to the fighting and bloodshed in sight, government intervention from the fledgling republic's leadership became all too urgent.

Approximately a dozen people lost their lives in the famed conflict between the Hatfield family and their adversaries, the McCoys. As many as twenty-five were killed in the Lincoln County War, which saw the birth pains to the legend of Billy The Kid. It is estimated more than 50 lost their lives in the years of conflict between the Regulator and Moderator factions of East Texas – more than the Hatfield-Mcoy, Lincoln County war,

Jaybird-Woodpecker War and the Earp Vendetta Ride combined. Only the Colfax County War of New Mexico seems to have topped it. The Lee-Peacock Feud – Occurring in Texas counties near the border between Texas and what is now the state of Oklahoma – saw roughly equivalent numbers of dead.

To be certain, this was an East Texas conflict. As you'll see in the latter chapters, Sam Houston and those in his administration very nearly waited too late to stop this destructive war. In the end, it was a number of events – including Annexation and a war with Mexico – that would bring about the ultimate end to this little-known period of violence in Texas History.

As previously mentioned, the Regulator-Moderator War saw the deaths of at least 50 people. Though some sources suggest the number could have been as high as 100 or even 200, the author finds these sources to be outliers, and most likely an inflated number meant to enlarge this already devastating conflict.

All of our todays will eventually become somebody's yesterdays. And many of their yesterdays are still yet to be our tomorrows. We are living history. May every person reading this – family or not – make it a period to remember in future generations. And may you not have to form a posse of your closest friends, family and confidantes to be remembered by history. Finally, please don't swindle people out of their land, money or property. Even in 21st century America, such an act is to be frowned upon.

–Edward Hancock II

1
RITTER'S THE NAME

Everett Ritter was born the son of Jesse Ritter, Jr, and grandson of Jesse Sr. There is some confusion as to the names of the wives of each Jesse but the line from Senior to Junior to Everett is well-documented, and fairly-well accepted as of 2021.

Born in 1810, Alabama would not hold young Everett long, as he would eventually make his way to Texas, serving in the Texas Revolution. He married Anna Goodwin, (Some documents record her as Hannah) daughter of Henry Goodwin and Sarah Jane Kennedy. Together, they would have at least nine children. Their eldest son, William, died as a result of his participation in the Civil War, though it's unclear if he died of disease or wounds suffered in battle. Everett's brother, Mark, died the same year as did William. Mark Ritter was a member of the Webster County Home Guards, who guarded Webster and Douglas County. There are two versions of the story of his death, each very different.

Nonetheless, he probably died while protecting his neighbors during a turbulent and deadly time. One story of his death, located on Findagrave, goes as follows: "During the war, men were allowed to go home every so often to get supplies and visit their families. While home on one of these visits, on the 18th of May, 1864, John Kirby, Mark Ritter & Hyram Potter were captured by a Confederate Regiment. They were called before a 'drum-head court martial court,' so called because a drum was used as a desk and the drumstick as gavel. The Confederates determined these young men were Union spies, and sentenced them to be executed. The three men thought this was just a scare tactic and considered it unlikely. They were marched to a spot just west of where a lumber yard stood for many years.

Three Confederate men were chosen as the executioners. After the soldiers dismounted, they took their pistols and faced the prisoners - the Captain gave orders to fire. John Kirby and Mark Ritter were both killed by a gunshot through their heart. Hyram Potter, however, knocked aside the pistol of the soldier facing him and ran for the underbrush. With the Confederates in pursuit, he made his escape, several shots passing through his clothing as he did so."

So, in the course of a year, Everett Ritter would lose both a son and brother to this great war.

Mark Ritter fathered at least 2 children before his execution. Thankfully, his bloodline did not die with him, as it did with so many in that horrible conflict.

William Ritter, Everett's son, died in November of the same year. While the circumstances of his death may remain a mystery, his service in Company C of the

28th Texas Cavalry is well-documented. Though it would be decades after the end of the Regulator-Moderator conflict, the Ritter family was a perfect example of what the American Civil War is always shown to be – truly brother against brother, family against family. The Regulator-Moderator war did not appear to be brother against brother. Families seemed to stick together and join one side or the other. Many did die. For what?

Of all the children of Everett Ritter, our momentary detours flow through two sons, Benjamin F. Ritter and James Henry Ritter. The former was the grandfather of actor and singer Tex Ritter. Tex was the father of the actor, John Ritter. James Henry Ritter lead to the author of this work, making John Ritter and the author third cousins twice removed. While the kinship might be different for others, perhaps some reading this find a similar kinship to these two talented stars whose light went out too soon.

However, it is Everett whose participation in the Regulator-Moderator War that gives our story its first participant.

When the conflict first broke out, Everett Ritter joined the Moderator faction. Most copies of the rolls list him as "Everett J. Ritter", perhaps suggesting a greater connection to his father, Jesse. However, every census record from the Texas Republic and United States lists him as "Everett Solomon Ritter" or simply "Everett S. Ritter". Regardless of his middle name or initial, this is the man that joined the conflict and the man that very nearly died in a conflict with yet another ancestor, one of the only known times two people within this story "met", or may have encountered each other. It is unlikely these two enemies shook hands and casually introduced themselves as the common ancestors of thousands yet to be born. As bullets passed among them, ,it is more likely neither man could have perceived of a moment when the descendants of their enemies would some day build a family together.

There are very few specifics as to Everett's personal participation in the conflict. He left no diary, journal or personal writings detailing this time in his life. There is a story where one family of Regulators, disgusted by what they saw as Regulator excesses switched sides to the Moderators. After this (perhaps in response to this. It is not entirely clear) a list of the twenty-five best Moderator fighters was prepared by the Regulator faction, headed by Sheriff Amon Lewellyn and a man known as Col. Jeff Cravens. One of the first names on this list of the most able fighters? Everett Ritter. These men were to be notified that they were to leave the area under threat of death, something few were unlikely to consider. Whatever else he was, Everett Ritter was one of the best fighters the Moderators had, probably due to his experience as a cavalryman in the Texas Revolution. He was there to put down what he saw as Regulator oppression of people just like him. He wasn't the first they'd "asked" to leave. He probably knew, had he failed to stand up, he was unlikely to have been the last. He wasn't just going to pull up stakes and leave the seemingly innocent unprotected. (It is during his time as a fighter in the Texas Revolution that the author speculates an encounter with a different ancestor may have occurred at some point. A bit more on that later.)

In August of 1844, Everett's fighting skills would be

desperately needed, as a fighting force of 65 Moderators gathered to face down an estimated 63 Regulators. Though the Moderator ranks eventually swelled to between 200 and 225, Everett's experience in battle – along with other veterans of the Texas revolution – acted as a counterbalance against the eagerness of lesser experienced, younger men spoiling far too hard for a fight. With the Regulators essentially surrounded by a vastly-superior force, a group of Moderators rode into a nearby town, bragging that Regulators were being killed in great numbers, alarming a group of more than 40 women who were wives, girlfriends, sweethearts, mothers and sisters of the Regulators. The women saddled up and rode unobstructed into the Regulator camp, only to find little more than a few injuries, cuts and scrapes. Riding back out of the redoubt, the women shouted at the members of the Moderator faction, "You fight like cowards!" Did they? They had a force of 3 to 4 times that of the Regulators. At any moment they could have crushed them. They could have waited until dark, sent 8 to 12 men in under the stillness of the twinkling stars and set the entire Regulator camp ablaze, forcing them to scatter from their cover, easy targets for the 200 to 225 Moderators. They didn't do that. Nor did they attack the women alarmed by the Moderator braggarts, who'd exaggerated the battle, for what purpose we'll probably never know. While he may not have been a leader per se, the Moderator faction benefitted from the experience of their veterans. They were patient. They simply waited the Regulators out, knowing there was nowhere for them to run.

It was August. It was East Texas. It was hot. Neither

side would have benefitted from a drawn-out conflict. Fight like cowards? Perhaps an argument could be made for that if a person wanted to. Perhaps it was simply the caution of veteran soldiers keeping the fighting from getting chaotic and confused, leading to even more deaths. That isn't cowardice. That's soldiering. These same women, and several others not in the original party, would also find themselves acting as scouts for the Regulator faction, counting on good old fashioned Southern Chivalry to prevent them from becoming targets. Later, a woman by the name of Helen Daggett Watt – Wife of one Regulator, sister to two others – would enter the Moderator camp and accuse multiple Moderators of firing on her. This accusation, while false, allowed the Regulators time to advance on the Moderator position. Battle began shortly thereafter. As it often does, the fog of battle created much of the undesired confusion. Several on both sides were felled by friendly fire.

After days of fighting, casualties on both sides compelled the combating forces to withdraw, marking an end to the last significant battle of the conflict. Soon, President Sam Houston would be forced to dispatch a contingent of militia to the area in order to quell the fighting.

By the end of 1844, a peace treaty of sorts had been signed ending – on paper at least – a conflict that matched or even bested the lengths of the Civil War, as well as each World War. While the actual death toll may never truly be known – as many were bushwhacked and killed in secretive, nefarious circumstances – the official death toll begins around 40 or 50 and only goes up from there.

Everett died in 1873, when the bloodshed of the Civil War was still fresh in the minds of Americans from all walks of life. But one can't help but wonder, as Everett Ritter breathed his last, did he lay in possession of any regrets for the lives he may potentially ended? Was there any thought of the conflict that preceded his final moments on earth by three decades. The conflict that shaped his life, as the civil war shaped the lives of his sons and his brothers. As previously stated, he left no written records from which we can draw any factual conclusions. As such, posterity can only speculate as to the musings of a man whose life led him to fight so many times, from one cause to the next.

It may be acceptable to speculate he entered the fighting with the right motives, wishing only to quell what he saw as bullying and intimidation tactics by members of the Regulator party. He was a participant in multiple battles and skirmishes and may have been present at lynchings or other such acts. Without greater evidence, this remains unclear. What remains clear is that he believed himself in the right, as did every other person involved in this conflict. Perhaps it is unfair to judge right and wrong, good and bad through the eyes of people far removed from the wild, untamed culture and society that bred men like Everett Ritter.

2
ROBERTS BEGINNINGS

The Roberts line in question is arguably the most interesting of the four lines to recount. Evidence points to a line that goes back to the 1600's, but said evidence is unreliable beyond a certain point, largely speculative and inadequately supported. What's interesting about this particular Roberts line is that it descends not from the author's maternal grandmother, whose maiden name was Roberts. Rather it descends from his grandfather, her husband who was not born a Roberts. As of 2021, the two lines have no discernable connection, despite the efforts of multiple researchers. The effort to find any connection, should it exist, continues. Both science and the Bible agree that all of humanity go back to a single man and woman. Somewhere there would exist a connection between these two lines. For now, it is unknown.

What we can say with great certainty, backed by documentation is William Elijah Roberts was the son of

Moses Fisk Roberts, known as "Dog" due to the constant presence of foxhounds near him. Moses was born July 9. 1803, in Davidson County, Tennessee. His father was Brigadier General Isaac Roberts, who served in the War of 1812 with the Militia of West Tennessee. After the Indian Massacre of August 1813, General Roberts was put in command at Fayetteville. Records indicate he assumed command October 4, 1813, of the first brigade to march south with General Andrew Jackson to punish the Native American belligerents. He and General Jackson disagreed over the length of time the recruits were to serve. General Roberts said it was three months, General Jackson said it was longer, leading to an angered exchange between them. The bitter argument led to a court martial for Brig. Gen. Roberts, effectively ending his military service.

According to papers kept by Isaac's granddaughter, he recorded his defense in writing, stating that he believed the men to be bound in service a mere 90 days and to capture, hold and imprison them per Gen. Jackson's orders would have violated their basic civil liberties as free citizens of the United States, thus subjecting him – in his view – to punishment and imprisonment himself. As such, he could not see fit to follow what he regarded as an unjust and essentially illegal order. In one communication, Roberts said he felt hurried into court, rendering him unable to supply testimony from a fellow officer, someone he regarded as "...my most material witness to prove that I used my best exertions to get the men to return..." He wrote to Judge John McNairy that he considered himself a scapegoat and a "lesson to others." Nevertheless, he was convicted and subsequently discharged from the military. Brig. Gen. Isaac Roberts passed away in 1816, aged just 55. Andrew Jackson would go on to be the 7th president of the United States.

Like General Jackson, Isaac had previously served in the Revolutionary War, each man at a very young age. It could be proposed that each man led a similar life, thus leading to a combustible situation by default. Born in approximately 1761, Isaac would have been a boy of 14 or 15 when hostilities broke out between the colonies and the British Empire in the 1770's. Andrew Jackson was a boy of just 13 when he was captured by British Forces. By the time war with Britain came to American shores a second time, Roberts was no longer a boy. He was a battle-tested, trained soldier with experience in the woods and hills in which he fought. Unlike Gen. Jackson. Isaac's career was taken from him, arguably under false pretense from trumped up charges by a superior more interested in affixing blame than finding solutions beneficial to everyone.

Moses "Dog" Roberts certainly seemed to inherit his father's fire, which he passed to his son in turn. Elijah was born in February of 1823. His mother was Amanda Grant. (Some sources say her last name was "Gant") The next decade or so is essentially undocumented for Moses, Elijah and the Roberts family. Elijah was a relatively young boy when the family left Tennessee. They arrived in Texas on Feb. 19, 1836, a few days before the Battle of the Alamo began in earnest. Upon arriving in Texas, Moses Roberts joined the Texas militia in their war for independence. He would serve under Captain James Chesser near San Augustine, losing his right eye in battle. As part of the struggle for independence, Moses would reach the rank of First Lieutenant. After the fight for independence was won, Moses "Dog" Roberts would again serve in the Texas Militia – with a missing eye – reaching the rank of Lt. Col. Throughout the rest of his life, he would be known as "Col. Roberts" to many of his contemporaries, friends and associates. He would eventually serve in the 4th, 5th and 6th congresses in the Republic of Texas, initially chosen to fill the seat left by Rev. Daniel Parker. Apparently, at that time, it was against the Texas Constitution for men of the clergy to serve as members of the legislative body, so Parker was never officially seated. Moses busied himself with political work, being rarely home despite the fact Amanda had died in 1839, just as tensions between the Regulator and Moderator factions were heating up. Moses would marry again a couple of years later. With his second wife, Nancy Murry, he had several more children.

Elijah Roberts joined the Regulator faction, Just 16 years old in 1839 when the first embers of war began to burn. Like his grandfather, his first taste of war came before he was, by today's legal standard, a man. As described earlier, he existed as one of the boys spoiling for a fight, joining the Regulators perhaps in hope of proving his mettle.

He participated in multiple skirmishes, meeting Everett Ritter in battle at least once, even trading shots with Ritter before the skirmish ended. Unlike the experienced leader Everett Ritter, it's unlikely a teenage Elijah Roberts was involved in leadership and decision-making. Roberts was described, by John W. Middleton, as "…materially in the support…" of Regulator efforts toward their brand of law and order. Middleton was a participant in this conflict himself and recounted knowing both Elijah and his father, Moses F. Roberts. Whether true or not, Middleton asserts that there may have been a Regulator involvement in the eventual election of Moses F. Roberts to the positions of political power he held within the Lone Star State. Moses' Regulator sympathies were well-documented by Middleton and others. What does "…materially in the support of…" mean? Was it just that? Material? Can we take the comment by the 21st century standard of literal and say he only supplied guns, ammunition and such? No. As stated above, Elijah was in the thick of it. He was a teenager by modern standards. More likely regarded as manly by standards of his day, he still would have been very unlikely to have any money, land or "materials" with which to support the efforts of his fellow Regulators. His "material" support was youth, manpower, bullets and guns, all his own.

It is very probable he was the most involved of every ancestor discussed in this entire book. In this instance, "materially involved" must mean greatly involved, if only as a soldier doing the actual fighting. It must be understood to mean Elijah Roberts, son of Moses "Dog" Roberts probably had blood on his hands. As a teenager, spoiling for the fight, he would have looked for opportunities. He would have potentially welcomed the opportunity to spill Moderator blood. Thankfully, he was unable to shed the blood of Everett Ritter or the other ancestors mentioned here.

Does this supposition – and that's what's it is – mean

Elijah was a bad man? No. It means he was a young man that fought for his beliefs, misguided as they might have been. He fought for his principles. He killed for his principles. He existed, young and unafraid, in a time when there were many reasons to cower in trepidation. He fought for what, in his mind, was the right cause, whether those of us in the 21st century agree with his decisions and motivations or not.

With the benefit of hindsight, his choices are very debatable. However, the main purpose of this book is not to debate motives and judgments from an era long past. Only to mention the potential and let each individual judge how they feel. Good, bad or indifferent, this story is to remind us where we come from and that the decisions made by our ancestors were not always easy and quite often not pretty.

Very little documentation exists on Elijah's specific and personal movements., save the aforementioned scant recollections of Middleton. We know certain battles, such as the final battle in 1844, would have been fought by nearly every Regulator in the area. Unfortunately, even the personal accounts do not list many specific interactions, save the aforementioned record of a small exchange of gunfire between young Roberts and his Moderator counterpart, Everett Ritter.

One small change, one right turn instead of left, one dodge when they should have shot back, one freeze when they should have ducked, one single fit of anger compelling them to run off half-cocked by themselves and millions born and unborn never exist. At any moment, so many of us were one bullet – one decision – away from not existing. The theme deliberately running throughout this entire story.

Elijah's young life could have ended before it truly began. Thankfully, it did not. Many reading this story now are alive because of one teenage boy's pure luck in violent battle. He was a teenager, untested and untried. He was a product of his era, when boys became men far earlier than they have to today.

Following the conflict. Elijah married Cornelia Jane Thomas. With her, he would have at least 4 daughters and 4 sons. Elijah's sister, Amanda M. Roberts, is the 3rd great-grandmother of the author, making Elijah a 3rd great-granduncle. The only known participant in this book to not be a direct ancestor. Nevertheless, his 8 children would have at least 23 children among them. (these 23 are actually among just 5 of the 8 children. One other appears to have been a life-long bachelor. Two others have confusing and conflicting information, still being researched as of this writing.) While the line further forward remains incomplete as of 2021, it is still known that those 23 children had children and grandchildren of their own. One man's death could have wiped out thousands of people still yet to be born.

Amanda M. Roberts, the direct ancestor of the author, was born on July 10th in the year 1839. Her mother passed away in September of the following year, leaving little Amanda with no chance of remembering the woman who'd given her life. Elijah was 16 when his mother died. He knew her. He ate with her. He laughed with her, cried with her. He likely mourned for her. One wonders did the big brother ever find time to tell little sister the stories, experiences and quirks of their mother, a woman with whom she shared a name. Did Moses

Roberts find time away from politics to share his own recollections of their first meetings, their courtship and the hard life that would take an impossible toll on young Amanda Grant Roberts. Too, Little Amanda was a baby during the Regulator-Moderator War's early days. A child of no more than 5 when it ended. What memories of that deadly time did she carry to her grave? This family connection is a reminder that it was not just the soldiers that suffered. As recounted in the tale of Everett Ritter, Mothers, wives, daughters, sisters and lovers suffered as well. In their own way, perhaps they suffered even more as the 19th century chivalric order of things rendered them largely helpless, save for the fact they were Texas-bred.

Amanda Roberts married William Martin Wilburn and would become the mother of no less than twelve children. Her daughter, Elizabeth Amanda Wilburn, married a man named Columbus Monroe and had at least two children, including Minnie Lee Monroe. Minnie was the great-grandmother of the author. She would give birth to three daughters and two sons, one of which died as a baby. It is from those children that the author, and many others reading this, descend.

A little side note: William Martin's parents were Lihue Tandy Wilburn and his first wife, Cynthia Brittain. Cynthia Brittain is the daughter of the very next ancestor explored in this book. Lihue Tandy Wilburn remarried, after his first wife's death, to Cynthia Jane Roberts, with whom he would have at least four more children. (The Wilburn and Brittain families of this lineage took the phrase "be fruitful and multiply" very seriously.) Cynthia Jane Roberts was a daughter of

Moses Fisk Roberts and his second wife, making her a half sister to Elijah and Amanda. Cynthia Roberts was born in 1846, two years after the official end of the conflict. Mere days before the outbreak of the Mexican-American War. There were *seemingly* no scores left to settle. By all appearances, unity of purpose had been achieved. A common enemy of Regulator and Moderator alike compelled many former combatants to fight side-by-side in a newer conflict, in a land far from the East Texas area where so many of their friends and loved ones had shed blood and perished in the effort to control frontier justice.

Had old wounds truly healed? No. But a common enemy goes a long way toward that end. When survival in a foreign land depends on the person standing next to you, old conflicts have a tendency to do one of two things. They either come boiling to the top endangering everyone around you or they get cast aside, whether permanently or temporarily so that, if nothing else, you may live to fight another day. With Elijah and Moses Roberts, it seems they survived the Regulator-Moderator War and the conflict with Mexico that followed not to fight, but to legislate and, as was common in those days, propagate.

3
THE CARRICO CONTRIBUTION

His name was Matthew Gillaspy Carrico. He was born in Kentucky in 1807 to William Carrico and an unknown wife. (It is believed her first name was Mary, but that's not fully proven.) He married Rachel Wilkerson and fathered numerous daughters and at least two sons, Winant Gillaspy and William David Carrico, the latter perhaps named for his grandfather. It is through William David's son, Carl, that the connection of the author descends. (More on that shortly.) The truth remains that very little else is concrete about Matthew Carrico's life beyond the fact he fought in the Texas war for independence, though there's no records of any wounds, as was the case with Dog Roberts. He's on a Tax roll from 1846 Texas, then found in the 1850 and 1860 Federal Census Records in Panola County. So, wherever he might have lived prior to the Regulator-Moderator conflict, he must have loved East Texas enough to stay. By the 1870 Census, Rachel is living alone with at least two children. Matthew's death date is believed to have been in 1862.

There is a story that he may have been at the Alamo, only to be sent as a courier or some such, in hopes of raising reinforcements. However, this story seems dubious and unlikely. Thus far, it remains unproven, due to lack of supporting documents. Nevertheless, anyone who can offer any documentation proving his alleged Alamo presence, if such documentation exists, would be most welcome. The author has seen 2 separate lists of combatants. Carrico's name does not appear on either, nor is there a name close enough to resemble the name Matthew Carrico. Another story suggests he received a land grant of 640 acres for his service "at Goliad." As there are two distinct battles of Goliad – one in 1835 and the more famous one lead by Col. Fannin in 1836 – it's impossible to say in which battle Carrico might have taken part. Despite schools often teaching no one survived the 1836 battle, there are several known to have survived that battle. Still, the author suggests the earlier battle is the more likely candidate if, indeed, our Matthew G. Carrico was present.

His service in the Texas struggle is widely-discussed and we can say he most likely fought for the freedom of what would become the Republic of Texas. He was brave and he was willing. As of 2021, he cannot be said to have been at the Alamo. He cannot be proven to have been at the 1835 battle of Goliad, as no accurate muster rolls were apparently taken. As to the 1836 Goliad Massacre, 400 to 450 Texians were killed, including James Fannin. Twenty-eight feigned death and escaped. Some of their names appear lost to history. Service in neither battle can be definitively backed up by documentation, outside of stories passed down by generations as of this writing.

Whether he fought at the Alamo, Goliad or not, his devotion to the new nation was real and would continue during the Regulator-Moderator war when he organized with a militia unit of 1,000 to 1,500 men (again, exact numbers vary among sources, but the most reliable tend to lean toward the 1,500 number. Though it's probable that number is both cavalry and infantry. The initial organization, of which Carrico was a part, numbered fewer than 50.)

Matthew Carrico is the main one those involved in researching this book cannot definitively say had personal contact with the rest. We know Sam Houston sent the troops to East Texas to encourage both sides to sit down, get along and talk things out. We know Matthew Carrico was among the troops dispatched by Houston to discourage either side from being combative while he was in their presence. We know he was a cavalryman in the Texas War for Independence, so he was an experienced soldier by the time he was called upon to join the force heading to East Texas. Still, there is no record that details any personal interaction between Matthew Carrico and those ancestors directly involved in the fighting between the two factions. The force of 1,000 to 1,500 was intimidating to the citizen warriors. The urgency for conflict seemed to subside with the presence of Houston's militia. To say nothing of the previously-mentioned conflict with Mexico that erupted in 1846. Just as a "perfect storm" of events took place to ignite hostilities, it seems the combination of a military presence and a more urgent battle on the horizon caused the flames of violence to subside, at least for the time being.

Carrico seems to have left no significant paper trail, aside from a limited number of census and tax records mentioned previously. No census records prior to Texas joining the United States where his movements could be adequately tracked. He is, in many ways, a ghost. We can say he was there, as was previously established. We can say he was part of the force that was organized to put an end to the fighting. We cannot say he ever fired a shot against them as it does not appear any major conflict arose between the Texas militiamen and the factions of Regulators or Moderators whose fighting they came to calm. Records prove that Houston's wish was to bring a force significant enough to dwarf those of the two factions combined. A true show of force. He expressed in at least one record that it was his belief that a strong force would keep guns silent, forcing the two factions to bend to his desire for peace. In a sense, he was right. As such, neither Matthew Carrico nor anyone with whom he served seemed to fire a shot in anger. The combined force of both factions would have been fewer than 500 people, at their respective peaks. Outnumbered many times over, the two sides reluctantly silenced their guns. It would be irresponsible, however, not to reiterate that, had anyone woke up with an urge for violence, Matthew Carrico could have been felled by a single bullet, potentially leading to a wider and much more bloody conflict, injuring and perhaps killing either Elijah Roberts, Everett Ritter or both. Thankfully, such a hypothetical battle never ignited.

As mentioned previously, Matthew G. Carrico

married Rachel S. Wilkerson. He was the father of many children, including William David Carrico. William David was born in 1852, years after the guns of both the Regulator-Moderator War and Mexican-American War had gone silent. He married Mary Charlotte Gary and would have many children. Possibly as many as ten, including Carl Leroy Carrico. Unlike his father, William David's life – tragic as it might have been – is well-documented. If available documents can be believed, he married in January of 1866, just 14 or 15 years of age. His bride was just 16 or 17 at the time. Their first born son, Winant Gillaspy Carrico, was born in January of 1867, so a "shotgun wedding" can be ruled out. In the 1880 Texas census, William and Mary are living in Panola County with 7 children listed. By 1900, William is listed as being in an asylum in Terrell, Texas, while his wife is living as a single woman, tending to the children still left at home. (The 1890 Federal Census was destroyed in a fire. While a few remnants do remain, no record of William's whereabouts has been found as of this writing. Some time between the 1880 and 1900 Census, William David Carrico entered into an asylum, for reasons as yet unknown.) William passed away in Terrell, Texas in 1935, nine years after his wife's passing. According to death records and available census records, it appears William never left the asylum. Whatever his emotional or mental disturbance, did he inherit it from his father? Or perhaps his mother? Did Matthew Carrico live with the scars of war, passing those scars to his son by his own actions or words or deeds? This can never be proven or disproven. Those who wish to can only speculate.

Carl Leroy – married Carrie A. Ritter, granddaughter of Everett, daughter of James Henry Ritter and his wife, Mary Elizabeth Ball. They would be the 2nd great-grandparents of the author. It is through their daughter, also named Mary Elizabeth, that the author descends. Mary Elizabeth Ball was the second wife of James Henry. Previously, he had been married to Mary's sister, Sarah. Sadly, Sarah died in 1869, likely giving birth to her only child, John Sampson Ritter. James Henry and Mary would have at least seven children, including Carrie Ritter.

With guns silent, the smoke of war cleared and the violence of the Regulator-Moderator war quelled, Matthew Carrico and his fellow soldiers returned to the life detailed in this brief chapter. Matthew largely disappears from the public record after this. There is a Matthew Carrico listed as part of the 50th Indiana infantry in the Civil War. The death date is in March of 1862, roughly the same as our Matthew Carrico. However, most records suggest our Matthew died in Panola County, Texas in 1862. (One document suggests 1863.) Are these two men the same? Unlikely, but unclear. Kentucky-born Matthew Carrico believed in freedom. When he arrived in Texas, he fought in the revolution. When called upon to stop fighting in the Regulator-Moderator War, he answered the call. Were his Kentucky roots crucial to his character? Did a fifty-something Matthew Carrico leave Texas only to die in another American struggle, perhaps having his body shipped back to East Texas for burial? For now, we must leave it as unlikely. However, it is the author's opinion that this was important enough to mention, as future generations will likely begin their own genealogical researches. In those searches, remember it is entirely possible for two men named Matthew to exist in the world. While less likely, it is entirely possible those two men were born or died on or about the same day, potentially both. Unlikely, but not impossible. The name Carrico is not as common as Smith or Jones. Without sufficient documentation, we cannot assume that any Matthew Carrico is our Matthew Carrico.

It is the author's hope that substantial documentation on this nearly invisible ancestor may one day become available. Hopefully, in the not so distant future, the author, or someone as deeply interested in this line, will uncover substantial truth as to the final moments of our Matthew G. Carrico. Until then, we can only acknowledge his name and the small, but brave, part he played in ending the fighting. Thank you, Matthew. Thank you for your role as part of the peacemaking force. Thank you for answering the call. Thank you for the things we can document and for those battles you may have fought that remain to be found. As it should be said to any soldier today, thank you for your service to *your* nation of Texas.

4
BRITTAIN SHADOWS

It is widely believed that part of this story began sometime in the 1730's, with the birth of one Nathaniel Brittain. In many ways, the story begins not with Nathaniel's birth but with his death. For our purposes, we begin merely with the fact that Nathaniel Brittain existed. For it is his descendant that first drew the author to the story you are now reading. Though this story is last in our tale (for reasons that will become clear as it unfolds) the story you are now reading – of familial involvements in the Regulator-Moderator War, began with the progeny of one Nathaniel Brittan. Without discovering a connection to this line, it's likely this book is never written. Without spending day after day chasing genealogical rabbits down the proverbial rabbit hole, this tale is book is never created. Without the random and unexpected discovery of one of Nathaniel's sons, this story is never told. Because Nathaniel Brittain existed, married and lived to have children, the author of this book can now share the very special place one of those children has in the family history that resulted in innumerable descendants yet to be born.

Born in the Carolinas, Nathaniel would marry Elizabeth Parks, daughter of Robert and Elizabeth Parks. Born a subject of the British Crown, Nathaniel Brittain enlisted in the 8th Virginia Regiment on March 4, 1776. (Coincidentally, March 4th is the author's birthday, albeit exactly 198 years after Brittain's enlistment.) There is some confusion on his date of death, as some records suggest Nathaniel died on October 17, 1777, in service to the colonial effort toward independence while at least one historian suggested Nathaniel Brittain may have died on October 17, 1776, mere months into his service. Some records at the genealogy website geni.com do seem to back up this 1776 theory. However, others in Ancestry's database suggest the 1777 date is accurate. Whether he died mere months in or one year hence, Nathaniel enlisted with the same hopes that countless others – the hopes of a future free to chart their own course, freed from the bonds of a tyrannical king ruling a people without representation in the governing parliament. Unfortunately, and like many others, he would not live to see his hopes come to their eventual fruition. Throughout this tale, the idea of "one bullet away from not existing" has been openly and bluntly reinforced. While not directly involved in this tale, Nathaniel's death in the Revolution reminds us that, had he not had children, his progeny is never – indirectly – involved in the Regulator-Moderator hostilities.

Before his unfortunate death, Nathaniel would father at least 8 children. His second son, George Brittain, served as a colonel in the war of 1812, later founding Harlan County, Kentucky. Another son, James, also served in the War of 1812, but details of his service or rank remain unknown. Nathaniel's son, William Martin was born in 1774. He would live until at least 1850. It is his line followed in order to connect the author to the conflict many years and miles away from that of William Martin's North Carolina birth.

The future Elder William Martin Brittain married Rosanna Wright in 1802, while still living in North Carolina. Through her father -- Revolutionary War Veteran, Captain John Wright III – Rosanna was a direct descendant of John Wesley Washington (1631-1677). John Wesley Washington was the great-grandfather of none other than George Washington, The First President of the United States under the Constitution. (Due to this relationship, the author is a 2nd cousin 9 times removed of George Washington.) Together, the couple would have at least 10 children, including Cynthia J. Brittain. Born in 1809, Cynthia was the 3rd child – and 2nd of William and Rosanna. She married Shelby County native Lihue Tandy Wilburn on November 13th, 1827. (Historically, they married when both families were in Alabama.) Others from the Wilburn family would marry into the Brittains. Lihue Tandy would marry a second time to Cynthia Jane Roberts. Intermarriage between neighboring families was commonplace in this era. Unlike today when anyone in Texas can speak to people in London, Madrid, Australia or any state in the United States at any given time via social media, there were no cars, no phones, no way to reach much further than your own proverbial neighborhood during their time. By modern standards, some might frown on these activities. To them it wasn't about desire, lust, sex or even love in some cases. In the Texas (and American) "wild", it was about survival. Thus was the case with the Brittains, Wilburns and others who arrived in Texas in the 1830's.

When the conflict between Regulator and Moderator factions broke out, several ministers and elders were vocal in relation to the conflict. Much of the word from the religious leaders was negative. One of the most vocal was, in fact, Elder William Brittain himself. He encouraged both sides to sit down and talk with each other, in the hopes of putting an end to the years of killing. He went as far as to chastise them from the pulpit, risking the ire of any number of men affiliated with the two warring factions. This never came to fruition, directly anyway. Again speaking hypothetically, Elder William Brittain could have been executed for his firebrand dissent. He could have been bushwhacked like so many others during the years of conflict that devastated the East Texas area. Perhaps due to the morality of the time, the Elder and his fellow ministers were not touched. Rather, they were allowed to rail virtually unhindered.

In 1847, a newspaper called the Niles Register gave a detailed account of an event that would, in the author's opinion, feel like an attempt to mete out a further portion of "Frontier Justice". One that would very directly affect not only Elder William Brittain but his family as well. In fact, details of this event were so profoundly evil that papers as far away as Cincinnati reported a version of events that, while not entirely in step with the more local records, does add some color to a horrible chain of events detailed in short order.

The Regulator-Moderator War "officially" came to an end in 1844 when Sam Houston, through a force of cavalry and infantry forced the leaders of the opposing factions to sign what amounted to a weak peace treaty. The treaty itself was difficult to enforce once the militia left, leading to occasional "dust ups", though any real fighting did stop with the signing of the treaty.

By the spring of 1847, hard feelings still existed in both camps. In the town of East Hamilton – Which had been changed from "Hamilton" as a town by that name already existed in Texas – there was a family named Wilkinson. Mr. Wilkinson – whose first name is unknown – had decided to host a wedding for his adopted daughter. By all accounts, Wilkinson was an old, grumpy man and probably a hog thief. He wasn't well-liked in the community, but a wedding was a grand affair in those days. One people would travel miles to attend. Unbeknownst to most of the town, crotchety, old Wilkinson still harbored a powerful grudge for what had happened to his family during this conflict. The wedding was to take place on April 22, 1847. The groom had expressed a desire to wait until June – in Texas -- But Wilkinson pushed for the April date. A local woman named Eddins was asked to bake the cakes. Some sources say she was in Wilkinson's employ. Others suggest she was simply known to Wilkinson as a woman in the area. Whatever the case, the wedding had a bride. The wedding had a groom. Now the wedding had a cook. All they needed now was someone to officiate. (Of note: the author has found numerous "Eddins" married into his family. As we do not know the identity of Mrs.

Eddins, nor any of her specific relatives. It is merely a compelling coincidence the author wished to point out, as it was relevant to this part of the story. As of 2021, no evidence connects the Eddins families married into the author's family to the Mrs. Eddins mentioned here. Hopefully, the full identity of Mrs. Eddins can be discovered in the future, leading to a final answer on this possible relationship.)

Upon baking the cakes, Mrs. Eddins left them in the smokehouse for safe keeping. The next morning, when she went to check on the cakes, she found the icing had been removed on every cake except one. That one was covered in custard. The other cakes were dark and discolored, but she did not have time to bake any more cakes. Instead, she opted to sprinkle them with sugar loaf and serve them to the guests.

Spottswood Sanders' family did not want to go to the wedding, as there had been disagreements between the two when Sanders accused Wilkinson of stealing some hogs – something he was reputed to do. (Wilkinson had been a Moderator. Sanders a Regulator.) After the family made the final decision not to go, Wilkinson had a veritable feast packed up and sent to the family. It was enough food to feed the entire family and every slave on their property.

Back at the wedding feast itself, the details become uncertain. Some say all the food was poisoned. Another version of the story suggested only the cakes had been poisoned. There is apparently agreement that the butter had been poisoned, so at least one thing other than the cakes likely contained some poison.

Spottswood Sanders' wife, Susan, was one of the first

victims to die, just a short time after her two sons, age 5 and 3. As she lay dying, she'd asked for the slaves to come in and say their goodbyes, not realizing many of them were dying and a couple had already died. Spottswood and his son, Francis, survived by crawling to the slop bucket, drank from it, vomiting up the poison, saving their lives.

Back at the party, Everyone was eating except the Wilkinson family. The poison – believed to be arsenic – didn't take long to begin working on those in attendance. Many dropped dead on the spot. Even some dogs and birds reportedly ate the food and died, howling and cawing as they die so. Others in attendance would linger for days. Still others would see their health drastically decline over the subsequent months, dying at what would have been considered an early age even in those times. It can't be definitively proven those who died young did so because of the arsenic. To the other end, the supposition cannot be truly disproven either. Elder William Brittain, who'd been asked to officiate the ceremony, died in 1850. Though this was just a couple of years after the Poisoned Wedding Supper, Elder Brittain was in his mid-70's at the time. If he'd ingested any of the poison, it's easy to assert it didn't help. Whether or not it hastened his death, however, cannot be established. More than likely, however, it was simply the fact of a man elderly by 19th century standards simply passing with time. Those people that survived the poisoning were heard shouting, ringing bells, and blowing horns, in the hopes of drawing attention to the crime unfolding at that very moment. People were dying and Mr. Wilkinson had killed them.

Mrs. Eddins, who had made the cakes, was poisoned, along with her son and a young slave girl. The poisoned butter left over from the meal was thrown out. The subsequent birds that ate of it died within minutes.

For Elder William Brittain, officiant of the nuptials, he entered the names of several members of his own family on the death page of a family bible. There exists five graves of Brittains in East Hamilton Cemetery with names but no dates. It is believed these graves belong to his family members. At least fifteen souls departed this world following the poisoning. Some sources say as many as twenty may have died. Another fifteen to seventeen were described as dangerously ill. According to articles written at the time, Wilkinson reportedly confessed to the poisoning, gleefully so. After being released from custody, Wilkinson remained afraid to leave his house for days. One evening, Wilkinson got it in his head to depart under the cover of darkness, hoping to escape punishment. Unbeknownst to him, several men were following him. They ran him down and lynched him. As so many had during the days of the Regulator-Moderator War itself, Moderator Wilkinson met his fate at the end of a vigilante horde's vengeful rope.

Elder William Brittain's life ended on September 16, 1850, aged 76. His wife, Rosey, outlived him by six years, dying in 1856, aged 72. William had outlived all but 2 of his siblings and had outlived other family members who had eaten the food at the poisoned wedding supper, including at least 2 children. He had made a life of speaking out against the conflict. Originally a part of the Predestinarian movement lead by Daniel Parker, (the very same Daniel Parker referenced in the Roberts chapter) William Brittain eventually adopted faith principles more in line with the Baptist teachings of his day, becoming a leader in his own right in the East Hamilton area, near Patroon, where he is buried.

Is his vocal opposition to the conflict the reason Wilkinson chose him to officiate the ceremony? Was he not necessarily chosen, but specifically among the targets of Wilkinson's ire? The entire event was believed to have been revenge on those who had opposed his Moderator faction. Was his choice of officiants deliberate? Sounds feasible. Daniel Parker – a vehement and vocal opponent – had died in 1844, so he couldn't perform the ceremony. But would a hog thief be willing to kill a man of God if he'd felt slighted by the Elder's harsh criticism? Whoever else Wilkinson was, he was apparently a man in possession of very few scruples. Without documented, legitimate evidence, all we can do today is add this question to the list of questions whose answer history is currently unwilling to reveal. We cannot say he deliberately targeted Elder Brittain and his family. However, we can readily assert with confidence that he would have lost no sleep over their possible demise.

Whatever his motives or intentions, Wilkinson was found and given the fate so many suffered during the Regulator-Moderator conflict. Being lynched without a trial by jury seems cruel to our society's modern sensibilities. Whether Wilkinson's fate was justified is up to each individual to decide. What we can say is killing people in cold blood, as Wilkinson had done, is wrong. Perhaps Wilkinson initially joined the Moderators with good intentions. In the end, however, he was nothing but a murderer. One that very nearly took the lives of Elder William Brittain and those from whom many of us descend. He succeeded in taking at least 15 lives. How many more were never to exist? We are unlikely to ever know. The conflict between the two factions was deadly. Boys as young as Elijah Roberts fought against veterans of the Texas Revolution. Judges and Sheriffs took sides, as did figures from various political strata. And, when everything was supposed to be settled and in the past, the cold dish of vengeance served death and sickness to innocents. Unlike the enemies Wilkinson had fought to destroy, Elder William Brittain's great crime was insistently calling on men of courage to embrace peace. Are the five unknown graves in East Hamilton Cemetery Brittain victims of the Poisoned Wedding Supper? As with so many other aspects of this family story, that question remains unanswered. For those of us who believe in a Benevolent Afterlife, perhaps one day we shall get the opportunity to meet with those who came before to help us answer questions the documents of this world seem willing to hide, at least for now.

5
CLOSING THE REVOLVING DOOR

This story is a very personal one. There are several books, websites and stories detailing the timeline and events of the Regulator-Moderator War far more detailed than you'll find here. The purpose of this book was never to tell the entirety of the war, it's prelude and its innumerable aftereffects. Neither was it the author's intent to retell the stories of Charles Jackson, Charles Watt Moorman, and the other pivotal leaders to the various factions. Too, unlike many other books, the purpose of this book was, in fact, a simple family record, as complete as it is possible to make it with currently available information. To tell the story (as completely as possible) of five men whose lives in the 1840s remain intrinsically linked, so long as the author, his mother, cousins, uncles, aunts and other family members continue to exist in increasing generations through time. One website suggests the number of direct descendants of just these families could number in the tens or hundreds of thousands as of 2021. Whether true today or not, one day the descendants of those depicted here may very well number in the millions. Perhaps more.

For the author, the search for information continues. As the chapter title suggests, researching genealogy is a bit like trying to close a revolving door to the author of this work. Round and round we will go, hoping that somewhere, someway, in some future point in time, documents can be uncovered enriching this story in numerous, possibly profound, ways. The documents we do have tell of well-traveled pioneers. People who chose to leave their distant places of birth in hopes of building a new future for themselves and their families. Without these actions, many of those same ancestors never meet the person with whom they would build a life and family. Throughout this story, a singular theme has been deliberately reiterated. That being the fact that, at any time, many people were one bullet away from not existing. Too, as was shown in the story on Elder Brittain, many were one bite of cake or too thick a spread of butter away from not existing. Revenge, they say, is a dish best served cold. Wilkinson apparently believed that, bided his time and attempted to eradicate those who'd once opposed him. He succeeded in killing at least fifteen to twenty. Dying with many of those fifteen to twenty was untold generations.

This story is to remind us to be grateful to those who came before. They were smart. They were strong. They were daring. They were brave and industrious. To theologically-minded, they would be termed blessed, highly favored. To others, they were just lucky. As this author sits pondering the similarities in those two perspectives, the realization strikes that, in fact, sometimes luck – or high favor -- is enough.

6
DOCUMENTS

There aren't many photos of the people depicted in this book. There are a couple, which will appear in this chapter, along with photos of historical markers and a singular military card. Last, the author as crafted a couple of genealogical trees to show the connections from the men depicted here, through to the generations. In the interest of privacy, the trees shown in this section begin with the men within this tale and end with the great-grandparents of the author. Every grandparent of the author has passed away, as has each of their siblings. That entire generation is gone. Still, it is the author's wish only to show the connection so many share, while not intruding on the privacy and security of others. Insert your missing generations within these trees. Find where you connect. And let the revelation be yours.

All we can do now is hope that the generations still with us have documents or stories we can record and pass down to future generations. Perhaps documents they've inherited from those who came before.

Tell those tales. For those on the younger side, ask the questions, listen to the stories, accept the documents, trees, files and photos passed down to you, sharing them with others that might be interested in their own search. In this age of technology, store the documents in multiple places and formats. Paper, electronic and even a bound form such as this one. It doesn't have to be a published book, nor do you have to be a published author. You simply have to be willing to assume the role of researcher, recordkeeper and storyteller. For those who desire to, the author hopes that this tale will be added to the stories passed down through the years.

(With exception of the two family trees created by the author to illustrate the connections, every image here was gathered from Ancestry and is considered to be in the public domain. The author does not own the images. But, in a sense, we all do. The people within belong to all of us after all.)

976.4
SP94t

Ritter, Everett S., 129

Spurlin, Charles D., Texas Veterans in the Mexican War...

Everett S. Ritter, veteran of the Mexican War. A very rare document proving the service of one of the ancestors depicted in this tale. Like others in this story (and many men of his day) Everett Ritter was no stranger to the battlefield.

Historical marker at the grave of Moses Fisk Roberts. He certainly left his mark on Texas.

Elder William Brittain, 1774-1850

Rosanna Wright Brittain, 1784-1856

Elder William Brittain and his wife, Rosanna, were present at the Poisoned Wedding Supper. The supper occurred in 1847. William died in 1850. They probably appeared very much as pictured here on the day of the heinous event. Their connection to the author gave birth to the story depicted here.

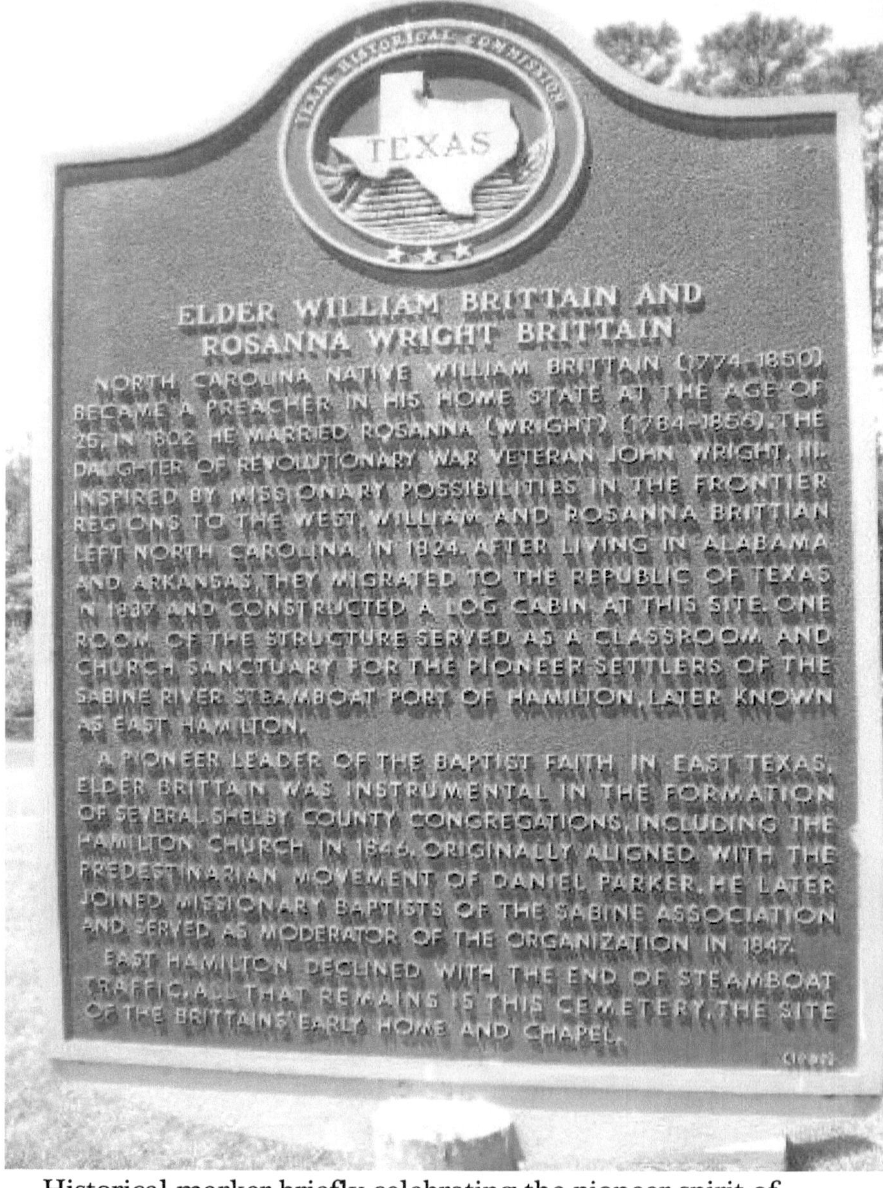

Historical marker briefly celebrating the pioneer spirit of William and Rosanna Wright Brittain. The marker can be found in Patroon, Shelby County, Texas.

William David Carrico, son of Matthew G. Carrico. While we have no photo of his father, William David's life is one of great tragedy. Whatever else he was in life, he certainly seems to have been a dapper dresser.

Mary Charlotte Gary Carrico
wife of William David

Not a very clear picture of Mary Charlotte Gary Carrico, but it is clear enough to see the care-worn face of the author's ancestor. The child in her lap is unknown. As she appears to be in her later years, it's possible the child is her grandchild. That's speculation at present.

This photo is believed to be Cynthia Jane Roberts pictured with her husband, Lihue Tandy Wilburn. This image was shared by multiple people via Ancestry.com, but it is unclear where the original came from or how it was identified as Cynthia Jane and Lihue Tandy. Cynthia Jane was the daughter of Moses Fisk Roberts and his second wife, making her the half-sister of Elijah Roberts and Amanda M. Roberts, ancestor of the author. Lihue Tandy had previously married another Cynthia. Cynthia Brittain was the daughter of Elder William Brittain and Rosanna.

Family Tree Carrico and Ritter families

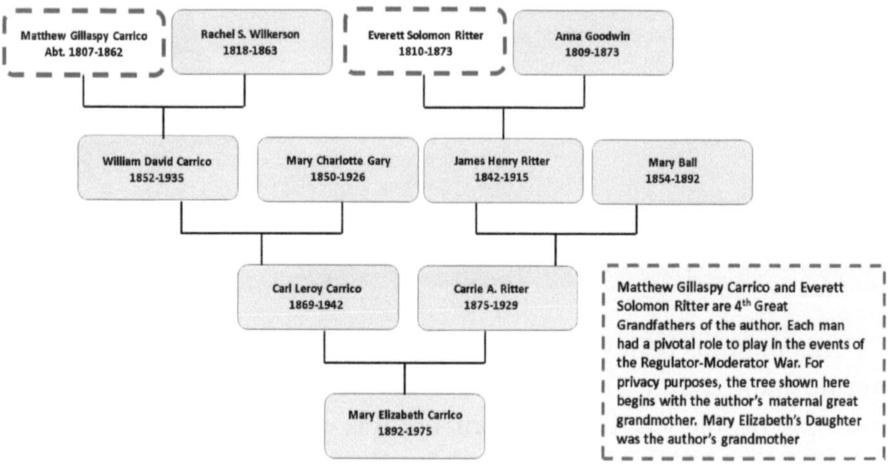

The Carrico and Ritter lines here connect to the author's maternal grandmother. Though Matthew Carrico is a bit of a genealogical ghost, Everett Ritter's line is fairly-well documented, right down to the author and his cousins Tex and John Ritter. Both Carrico and Ritter were veterans of the Texas war for Independence. If one or both of these men had died, during their lives of war and conflict, everyone below them on the chart (and every person from whom they and their siblings sprang) is never born. They were brave men. But they were, at times, dangerous men. Thankfully, they lived so that we can continue to research their stories.

Family Tree Brittain and Roberts families

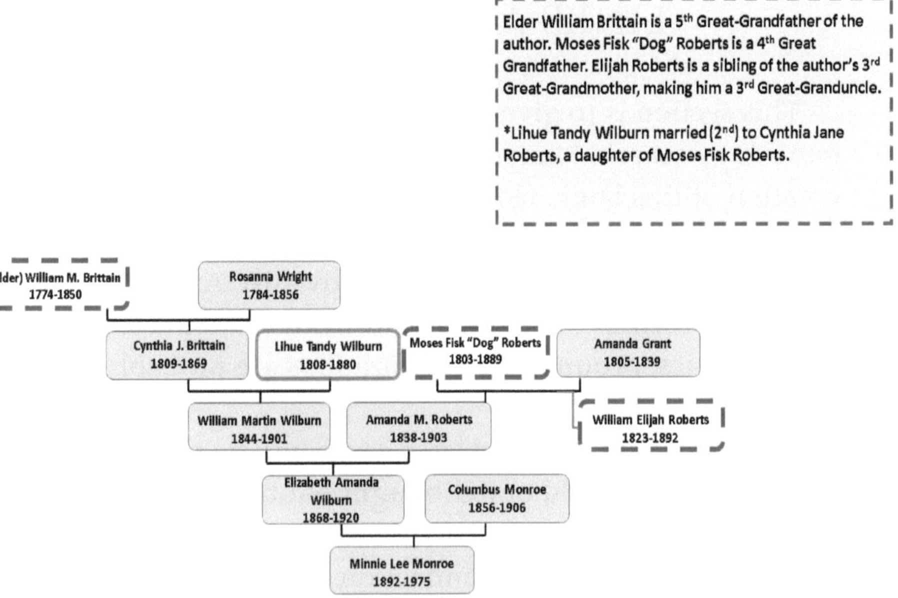

The Roberts and Brittain lines shown here connect to the author's maternal grandfather. As explained earlier, both grandparents have a Roberts line. The line shown here ends with the author's great-grandmother, Minnie Lee Monroe. Her son was the author's maternal grandfather. While William Elijah Roberts is not a direct ancestor his involvement was integral to the story. Interestingly, it is through Minnie Lee Monroe's ancestor, Rosanna Wright, that the author and many others descend from a common ancestor of George Washington, First President of the United States under the Constitution.

7
LINKS AND WEBSITES

This section is to give the reader a start on their own genealogy search. Many of these are websites used in the creation of this book. However, some of the websites here are simply beneficial to genealogical searches in general. In no way is this an exhaustive list. As the author is based in the United States, international sites, communities, groups and organizations are probably unfamiliar.

As time passes, new websites come into being. Too, existing websites fold or get bought out by others and rebranded. The websites listed here are publicly available via an internet connection. Again, this list is not exhaustive. There are literally hundreds of websites with tools that might aid in your genealogy search. A number of great websites have potential benefits to your search, though they may not be listed here. Others may portend to be beneficial but remain unmonitored, leading to unreliable information. Above all, the author recommends attending local workshops and watching videos from professionals who have spent years helping people find their long lost relatives. As an unconventional method for finding ancestors and cousins from a certain era or culture, you could attend Renaissance Festivals, Celtic Fests, book talks or signings by certain non-fiction authors and other such cultural events. This has, occasionally, lead the author to a previously-unknown connection. While family reunions seem to have fallen into relative obscurity, meeting family members, reading or perhaps starting a family news letter can lead to numerous stories, photos and resources.

Professional genealogists can cost a lot of money, but are generally worth it if you have the money to spend. When all else fails, start with a general search engine. Use caution, no matter which website you visit. Not every "fact" you will find will apply to your specific ancestor or relative. To use the words of a legendary political figure, "Trust but Verify":

Ancestry.com
Geni.com
Usgenweb.org
23andme.com
Genealogybank.com
Familysearch.com
Famouskin.com
Wikitree.com
Myheritage.com
Findmypast.com
Fold3.com
Billiongraves.com
Findagrave.com
Newspapers.com
JewishGen.com
DAR.org
Tudorplace.com
Billiongraves.com
Genealogy.com
Cyndislist.com
Ancestralfindings.com
Familyhistoryfanatics.com
WieWasWie.nl/en/
Loc.gov
Britannica.com

ABOUT THE AUTHOR

Edward Hancock II is primarily a fiction author. A life-long obsession with family history and genealogy compelled him to use his research and writing talents to compose a series of family-related stories. The first, a compilation of his paternal grandfather's letters, written during World War II, continues to reach new fans across the globe. When not spending time with his four-legged brood, he is busily working on multiple projects, both fiction and non-fiction.

www.ingramcontent.com/pod-product-compliance
Ingram Content Group UK Ltd.
Pitfield, Milton Keynes, MK11 3LW, UK
UKHW040028200726
13854UKWH00001B/420